YOUR KNOWLEDGE HAS

- We will publish your bachelor's and master's thesis, essays and papers

- Your own eBook and book - sold worldwide in all relevant shops

- Earn money with each sale

Upload your text at www.GRIN.com and publish for free

Bo Tian

Bouncing Bubble: A fast algorithm for Minimal Enclosing Ball problem

GRIN Verlag

Bibliografische Information der Deutschen Nationalbibliothek:

Die Deutsche Bibliothek verzeichnet diese Publikation in der Deutschen National-
bibliografie; detaillierte bibliografische Daten sind im Internet über http://dnb.d-
nb.de/ abrufbar.

Imprint:

Copyright © 2012 GRIN Verlag GmbH
Druck und Bindung: Books on Demand GmbH, Norderstedt Germany
ISBN: 978-3-656-32699-1

This book at GRIN:

http://www.grin.com/en/e-book/204869/bouncing-bubble-a-fast-algorithm-for-
minimal-enclosing-ball-problem

Bouncing Bubble - A fast algorithm for Minimal Enclosing Ball problem

Tian Bo[1]

Fig 1 An example of MEB covering German cities, $\epsilon = 10^{-4}$, solved in 0.025s

Abstract

In this paper, a new algorithm for solving MEB problem is proposed based on new understandings on the geometry property of minimal enclosing ball problem. A substitution of Ritter's algorithm is proposed to get approximate results with higher precision, and a 1+ϵ approximation algorithm is presented to get approximation with specified precision within much less time comparing with present algorithms.

With the new 1+ϵ approximation algorithm , A large case d=2048, n=128k, ϵ=10^{-6} can be solved in a few minutes, which has not been done with previous solvers.

1. Introduction

Also known as bounding sphere problem or Smallest Enclosing Ball problem, Minimal Enclosing Ball (MEB) problem is to find out the minimal enclosing ball for a given set of points $P \subset \mathbb{R}^d$. The MEB problem was well studied for its large number of applications, which include computational graphic, high dimensional data mining etc. See more reference in Fischer [1], or Kumar [2].

Data mining techniques such as clustering, nearest neighbor searching usually involves MEB problems in high dimensions, which become very time consuming or even impractical to be

---

[1] Freelancer; Kaspar-Kerll Str. 4a. 81245, Munich, Germany; tmsfld@googlemail.com

solved for traditional exact solver such as Welzl's method [3] or approach of Gärtner et al.

Ritter's solution [6] is an attempt for providing a bounding sphere. The fascinating thing of Ritter's approach is its simplicity of implementation and its short execution time. However, it provides only very coarse result with around 15% error. In comparison, the substitution provide results with 1%~2% error.

Bădoiu et al introduced an approach that apply Second Order Cone Programming (SOCP) on a subset of the data set (referred as core set) to get an approximate result, any point outside 1+ε approximation will be added into the core set until all points reside in the 1+ε approximation. This approach yield to a computational complexity of $O\left(\frac{dn}{\epsilon^2} + \left(\frac{1}{\epsilon}\right)^{10} \log \frac{1}{\epsilon}\right)$ [5]. Kumar et al improved this approach by solving the problem with incremental precision [2]. The result computational complexity is $O\left(\frac{nd}{\epsilon} + \frac{1}{\epsilon^{4.5}} \log \frac{1}{\epsilon}\right)$.

Another noticeable contribution is the approach by Fischer et al. They proposed an exact solver with $O(nd^2)$ complexity [1].

These two algorithm are quite successful since they were proposed. However, alternative approaches to solve MEB problem can be even more efficient in practice.

Instead of using core-set, new approach maintains a expanding ball (referred as "Bubble") that is always smaller than MEB, and inflates it until its 1+ε ball contains all points. In each inflation, only one point is involved, so that the computation is very minimal. The algorithm is called Bouncing Bubble algorithm because during the inflating process, the bubble is moving around like bouncing among the points. With this new algorithm, MEB 1+ε approximation can be solved in $O(nd) + O\left(\frac{d}{\epsilon^2}\right)$.

This paper is organized in this way: the background of the problem and related work will be introduced in section 2. Some mathematic observations on the MEB problem will be discussed in section 3. Section 4 will present algorithms and some discussions on the behavior of the algorithms. In section 5, a more sophisticate algorithm to cope with arbitrary precision and exact solution is presented. And finally experimental results and conclusions will be given in section 6.

2. Related Works

In this section, some previous work will be briefly described. Since this is not a review paper, only most related works are listed here.

Ritter's bounding sphere

Ritter proposed a simple algorithm to find a "bounding sphere" around data set **P**. The algorithm can be described as follows:

1. Pick a point **x** from **P**, search a point **y** in **P**, which has the largest distance from **x**;

2. Search a point **z** in **P**, which has the largest distance from **y**. set up an initial ball **B**, with its centre as the midpoint of **y** and **z**, the radius as half of the distance between **y** and **z**;

3. If all points in **P** is within ball **B**, then we get a bounding sphere. Otherwise, let **p** be the point outside the ball, which has distance d from the boundary of **B**. Move the centre of **B** towards p by d/2, and increase radius by d/2 to get a new ball.

The beauty of Ritter's algorithm is its simplicity. With only 3 walks through the data set, it produce a reasonable small bounding sphere.

In brief, Ritter's algorithm tries to find a ball as large as possible (As shown in step 1,2, which was first introduced by Egecioglu and Kalantari in [7]), and then enlarges it further more to cover all points in **P**. The final step ensure all points in **P** is enclosed by the given ball. In this paper, step 3 will be referred as "Ritter's enclosing approach", and will be used as final step for some proposed algorithms.

Bǎdoiu 's Core set based 1+ϵ approximation

Core set was introduced by Bǎdoiu et al. The brief idea of the algorithm is to find a subset of the point set, and compute the MEB of the subset as a solution. It can be detailed as follows:

1. Pick a point **x** from **P**, search a point **y** in **P**, which has the largest distance from **x**;

2. Search a point **z** in **P**, which has the largest distance from **y**. Initial core set as {y,z} and set an initial ball **B**, with its centre as the midpoint of **y** and **z**, the radius as half of the distance between **y** and **z**;

3. If all points in **P** is within ball (1+ϵ)**B**, then we get a bounding 1+ϵ approximation. Otherwise, let **p** be the farthest point from the centre of **B**, add **p** into core set; Compute a new ball **B** to be MEB of the core set. Repeat step 3 until 1+ϵ approximation is obtained.

In fact, the first two steps are the same with which was used in Ritter's algorithm. In step 3, the author use SOCP to obtain MEB of core set.

Kumar's Core set based 1+ϵ approximation

Kumar's improvement is to compute a core set start with coarse precision (say, $2^k \epsilon$), and then compute core set with $2^{k-1}\epsilon$, and so on and so forth, until finally with precision ϵ. In this way, the size of core set is minimized and therefore computational complexity is also minimized. The result computational complexity is .

As we can see, since these 1+ϵ approximation requires choosing a subset of data and applying SOCP on it, the implementation become more complex.

3. Preliminary

This section discuss some basic geometry property of MEB problem and the property of a "Bubble".

Let's denote B(**C**, r) as a d-dimensional ball, where $\mathbf{C} \in \mathbb{R}^d$ is its centre and $r \in \mathbb{R}_+$ is its radius. For simplicity reason, we denote B_i as $B(\mathbf{C}_i, r_i)$ when there would be no confusion.

Let $B(C_*, r_*)$ be the MEB of point set $P \subset \mathbb{R}^d$. As proved in [3], $B(C_*, r_*)$ exists and is unique.

We call ball $B(C, r)$ a "Bubble" when it satisfy the inequality $\|C_*C\|^2 + r^2 \leq r_*^2$. See Fig 2.

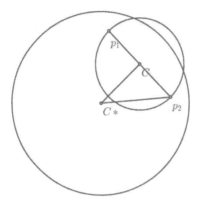

Fig 2 Definition of a bubble

A bubble is basically a ball that the MEB could cover at least half of it. According to the definition, any point $p \in P$ is a bubble with its radius equals to zero. MEB itself is also a bubble.

Lemma 1. Let P_1, P_2 be two points inside $B(C_*, r_*)$, $P_1 \in B(C_*, r_*)$, $P_2 \in B(C_*, r_*)$. Let $B(C, r)$ be a ball where C is the midpoint of P_1P_2, $C = \frac{1}{2}(P_1 + P_2), r = \frac{1}{2}|P_1P_2|$, then $B(C, r)$ is a bubble.

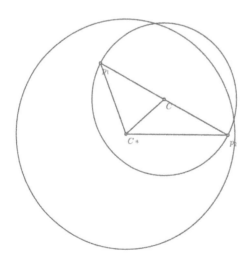

Fig 3 Bubble construction from two points

Proof:

$$\|C_*C\|^2 + r^2 = \|C_*C\|^2 + \|C\,P_1\|^2 = \|C_*C\|^2 + \|C\,P_2\|^2$$

One of the following inequalities must be true

$$\begin{cases} \|C_*C\|^2 + \|C\,P_1\|^2 \le \|C_*\,P_1\|^2 \\ \|C_*C\|^2 + \|C\,P_2\|^2 \le \|C_*\,P_2\|^2 \end{cases}$$

Thus

$$\|C_*C\|^2 + r^2 \le \max(\|C_*\,P_1\|^2, \|C_*\,P_2\|^2) \le r_*^2$$

Recall that the first two steps of Ritter's algorithm is to find a big enough ball, which is actually to find a big enough bubble.

As an extension to Lemma 1, we have:

Lemma 2. Let S be a subset of P, $S \subset P$, B(C, r) is the MEB of S, then B(C, r) is a bubble of P.

Proof:

According to lemma 3.1 in Kumar 2003, let hyperplane L pass through C and be perpendicular to C_*C, there exists a point $p \in S$, p resides on the half space farther from C_*. Thus

$$\|C_*C\|^2 + r^2 \le \|C_*\,p\|^2 \le r_*^2$$

This lemma shows that core set based algorithm can be considered as a variant of Bouncing bubble algorithm which construct inflating bubble in a different fashion.

Lemma 3. Let $B(C_i, r_i)$ be a set of bubbles, $1 \le i \le n$, then B(C, r) is also a bubble, where $C = \frac{1}{n}\Sigma C_i$, $r = \sqrt{\frac{\Sigma r_i^2}{n}}$.

Proof:

Let $d_i = C_* - C_i$

$$\|C_*C\|^2 = \left| C_* - \frac{1}{n}\Sigma C_i \right|^2$$

$$= \left| \frac{1}{n}\Sigma(C_* - C_i) \right|^2$$

$$= \left| \frac{1}{n}\Sigma d_i \right|^2 = \frac{1}{n^2}\sum_{ij} d_i \cdot d_j$$

$$\le \frac{1}{n^2}\sum_{ij} \|d_i\|\|d_j\| = \left(\frac{\Sigma_i |d_i|}{n} \right)^2$$

$$\le \frac{\Sigma_i |d_i|^2}{n}$$

Thus it's obvious that

$$\|C_*C\|^2 + r^2 \leq \frac{\sum_i |d_i|^2}{n} + \frac{\sum_i r_i^2}{n} = \frac{1}{n}\sum_i \left(\|d_i\|^2 + r_i^2\right) \leq r_*^2$$

This lemma shows that an affine combination of bubbles is also a bubble. This lemma is listed here only for completeness, it's not referenced in the rest of the paper.

Lemma 4.   Let $B(C_1, r_1)$ be a bubble, $p \in P$, $p \notin B(C_1, r_1)$, Let $B(C_2, r_2)$ be the smallest ball witch go through p and covers at least a hemisphere of $B(C_1, r_1)$. Then $B(C_2, r_2)$ is also a bubble.

Proof:

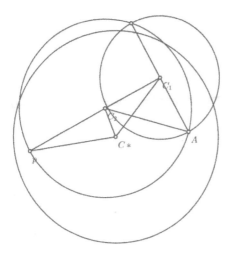

Fig 4 Bubble Inflation

As shown in above figure, obviously C_2 is on pC_1.

Let A be a point on the intersection of boundary of $B(C_1, r_1)$ and $B(C_2, r_2)$.

If $\angle pC_2C_* \geq \pi/2$, then

$$\begin{aligned}
\|C_*C_2\|^2 + r_2^2 &= \|C_*C_2\|^2 + \|pC_2\|^2 \\
&\leq \|pC_*\|^2 \\
&\leq r_*^2
\end{aligned}$$

if $\angle pC_2C_* \leq \pi/2$. then

$$\begin{aligned}
\|C_*C_2\|^2 + r_2^2 &= \|C_*C_2\|^2 + \|C_2A\|^2 \\
&= \|C_*C_2\|^2 + \|C_2C_1\|^2 + \|C_1A\|^2
\end{aligned}$$

$$\leq \|C_*C_1\|^2 + \|C_1A\|^2$$
$$= |C_*C_1|^2 + r_1^2$$
$$\leq r_*^2$$

Thus the new constructed ball is also a bubble.

Lemma 5.   Let $B(C_2, r_2)$ be the bubble constructed from bubble $B(C_1, r_1)$ and point $p \in P$ according to Lemma 4. We have

$$r_2 = \frac{1}{2}\left(\alpha + \frac{1}{\alpha}\right)r_1 > r_1$$

$$C_2 = \frac{1}{2}\left(\left(1 + \frac{1}{\alpha^2}\right)C_1 + \left(1 - \frac{1}{\alpha^2}\right)p\right)$$

Where $\alpha = \frac{\|pC_1\|}{r_1} > 1$

according to Pythagorean theorem

$$\|C_2A\|^2 = \|C_2C_1\|^2 + \|C_1A\|^2$$

Thus

$$r_2^2 = (\|pC_1\| - r_2)^2 + r_1^2$$

Solve this equation, the lemma is proved.

Let $B(C_1, r_1)$ be a point in P, i.e. $C_1 \in P$, $r_1 = 0$, then we have Lemma 1. Thus Lemma 1 can be considered as a special case of Lemma 5.

Lemma 4 and Lemma 5 show that a larger bubble can be constructed from an existing bubble and a point outside the bubble. These two lemmas form the foundation of our algorithm presented in this paper.

4.   Basic Bouncing Bubble algorithm

Algorithm 1.   Basic Bouncing Bubble
  Procedure BouncingBubbleBasic(**S**)
  begin
      $B_1 :=$ any point $p \in S$;
      for i := 1 to 2
          for each $p \in S$
              if $\|pC\| > r$
                  construct new Bubble B_{i+1} according to Lemma 5
      Call Ritter's enclosing approach;
  end;

This algorithm is easy to be implemented as there is no LP, nor SCOP. It uses only simple iterations to compute a approximation. Thus the computational complexity is minimized. In fact, it walks through the data set only 3 times (same as Ritter's algorithm does).

As simple as it is, in all cases we tested it produces better results than Ritter's approach. In most cases, the error is less than 2%, where Ritter's approach usually result in around 15% error. Thus we propose this algorithm as a substitution of Ritter's algorithm.

Since Ritter's algorithm is also based on the construction of a bubble (according to Lemma 1), we can consider this algorithm as an extension of Ritter's original.

According to Lemma 4, it's easy to see that the radius grows very fast when the bubble is small. As we can see in Fig 5 which shows a plot of $\frac{1}{2}\left(\alpha + \frac{1}{\alpha}\right)$ against α. Another merit we have is that the probability of finding a new outside point is also larger as the bubble is small. This property ensures that we can get an approximation in relatively short time.

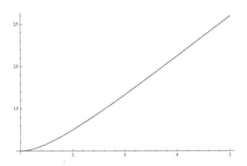

Fig 5 plot of $\frac{1}{2}\left(\alpha + \frac{1}{\alpha}\right)$

The inflation slows down only when the bubble become close to MEB. At that time α is close to 1, $\frac{1}{2}\left(\alpha + \frac{1}{\alpha}\right) \rightarrow 1 + \frac{1}{2}(\alpha - 1)^2$ is also very close to 1, and finding a new outside point become harder.

To estimate the error of the result, let P be a uniformly distributed data set, B(C, r) be a bubble, $\gamma = |CC_*|$, after a new point is examined(could be inside or outside B), we have a new bubble(could be the same ball when new point is inside B) where:

$$E(r) = \frac{1}{V_*} \int\limits_{p \in MEB, p \notin B} \frac{\|pC\|^2 + r^2}{2\|pC\|} dv + \frac{V_{B \cap MEB}}{V_*} r$$

$$E(\gamma) = \frac{1}{V_*} \int\limits_{p \in MEB, p \notin B} \|C'C_*\| dv + \frac{V_{B \cap MEB}}{V_*} \gamma$$

E(r), E(y) can be estimated using numeric integration. The following plot shows E(r)/r against r for dimension 3, 32 and 256.

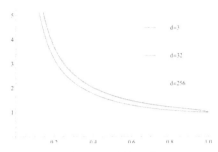

Fig 6 Acceleration in different dimensions

As shown in Fig 6, it's little bit surprising that the acceleration in high dimension is higher than those in low dimension. This is because points tend to accumulate close to the surface in higher dimensions thus the probability of finding a outside point is proximately $1 - \left(\frac{r}{r_*}\right)^d$, which is close to 1 for high dimensional data set when r<r*.

However, the differences among higher dimensions become very minimal (for instance, the difference between d=32 and d=256 is almost indistinguishable).

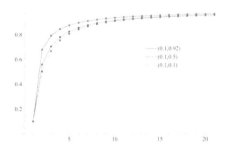

Fig 7 Convergence from different start points (d=8)

Use E(r) and E(y) for next iteration, we can get a view of how radius grows. The first observation is that the position of initial ball is not important because it converges very fast. Fig 7 demonstrates the process. In this demonstration, without losing generality, we set r*=1. The iterations start from 3 different locations (represented by radius and distance between C and C*).

As we can see, the iteration is not sensitive to the initial position. The difference become indistinguishable after only 20 iterations.

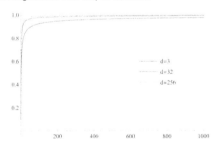

Fig 8 Convergence in different dimension

As we already knew, it's easier to get an approximate result for higher dimensional point set. As shown in Fig 8.

Based on the observation mentioned above, we know that one can expect a good result from this algorithm for large high dimensional data set. But for small data set in low dimension space, we may need to add more iterations in step 2.

5. Pruning Bouncing Bubble algorithm

As we discussed, Basic Bouncing Bubble algorithm is simple to implement and works well in low precision situation thus can be applied in many applications. However, there are two major reasons to develop a more sophisicated version.

First, it's always good to know the boundary of error. Basic version produce good results in most cases, but there is no way to tell the exact error. Second, when we need a more precise result, say $\epsilon = 10^{-4}$ or higher, even for very large high dimensional data set we have $nd \ll 1/\epsilon^2$, we have to walk through data set repeatedly thus cause longer execution time.

Definition: $1+\epsilon$ approximation

We will refer a ball as $1+\epsilon$ approximation to MEB of set P, when its radius is less than r_*, and its $1+\epsilon$ expansion covers set P.

Lemma 6.   There exists a bubble constructed from set P, which is a $1+\epsilon$ approximation to MEB of set P.

Proof:

Let $B(C_0, r_0)$ be an arbitrary point in P.

If there is no point $\mathbf{p} \in P$, such that $\|\mathbf{p} - C_i\| > (1+\epsilon)r_i$, then $B(C_i, r_i)$ is the $1+\epsilon$ approximation to MEB of set P.

If there is a point $\mathbf{p} \in P$, and $\|\mathbf{p} - C_i\| > (1+\epsilon)r_i$, then we can construct a new bubble from B_i and $\mathbf{p}$ according to Lemma 5.

In this case we have:

$$r_{i+1} = \frac{1}{2}\left(\alpha + \frac{1}{\alpha}\right)r_i$$

where $\alpha = \frac{\|pC_i\|}{r_i} > 1 + \epsilon$

$$\Rightarrow \frac{(r_{i+1} - r_i)}{r_i} = \frac{1}{2}\left(\alpha + \frac{1}{\alpha}\right) - 1 > \frac{\epsilon^2}{2(1+\epsilon)}$$

This show each time when we find a new point, the radius of bubble will increase at least $\frac{\epsilon^2}{2(1+\epsilon)}$ times.

As r_*, r_0 are finite numbers, this leads to a conclusion that this process will come to a end after

$\frac{r_*}{r_0} \frac{2(1+\epsilon)}{\epsilon^2}$ operations.

This lemma suggest a new approach to get 1+ε approximation other than the algorithm proposed by Bădoiu [5] or Kumar [2].

Algorithm 2. 1+ε Bouncing Bubble Algorithm
  Procedure BouncingBubble1PlusEpsilon(**S**, ε)
  begin
    do
      for each **p** ∈ **S**
        if $\|pC\| > (1+\epsilon)r$
          construct new Bubble B(**C**,r) according to Lemma 5
          changed = true;
    while(changed);
    Call Ritter's enclosing approach;
  end;

Another observation is that after each walk through the entire data set, most points will be always inside the bubble, thus we can prune them off to avoid useless computation.

Lemma 7.   Let ball B(**C**, r) be a 1+ε approximation to MEB of set **P**, any point inside B(**C**, (1-ε)r) will be inside B(**C***, r*).

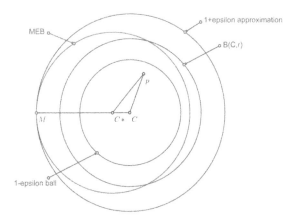

Fig 9 1-ϵ ball

Proof: As shown in Fig 9 1-ϵ ball, $\|p - C\| < (1-\epsilon)r$, according to triangle inequality,

$$\|p - C_*\| \leq \|p - C\| + \|C_* - C\|$$
$$= \|p - C\| + \|M - C\| - \|C_* - M\|$$
$$< (1-\epsilon)r + (1+\epsilon)r - r$$

$$= r$$
$$\leq r_*$$

Since only those points on the surface of MEB will affect the size of MEB, thus this lemma shows that when a 1+ϵ approximation was obtained, we can eliminate all the points inside the 1-ϵ ball to get a small point set P' for further processing.

Algorithm 3. Pruning Bouncing Bubble algorithm

> **Procedure** PruningBouncingBubble(S, ϵ)
> **begin**
> **do**
>> **for each** p $\in$ S
>>> **if** $\| pC \|$ > r
>>>> construct new Bubble B(C,r) according to Lemma 5;
>>
>> $$\epsilon' = \max_{p \in S}(\|pC\|) \frac{1}{r} - 1;$$
>>
>> **for each** p $\in$ S
>>> **if** $\| pC \|$ <(1-ϵ')r
>>>> drop **p** from S;
>>>> changed = true;
>> **while**(changed);
>> call BouncingBubble1PlusEpsilon(S, ϵ);
> **end**;

This algorithm is supposed to be very adaptive to different distributions: if the points in the data set are concentrated in the centre area, they will tend to be pruned; if they are concentrated in the surface area of MEB, each of them will be very likely contributed to inflate the bubble.

Time complexity

The pruning phase takes approximately O(nd) time. After pruning, the remaining points are closed to or exactly on the surface of MEB. There is constant probability to encounter a surface points which will contribute to the radius growth by at least $\frac{\epsilon^2}{2}$. Thus the time complexity of the final step is $O\left(\frac{d}{\epsilon^2}\right)$.

So we have the time complexity for algorithm 3 as $O(nd) + O\left(\frac{d}{\epsilon^2}\right)$. When ϵ is small enough, the size of data set becomes trivial.

Extension for exact solver

Algorithm 3 can be easily extended to an exact solver by replace last step to an off-the-shelf exact solver (Fischer's algorithm, for instance).

Implementation

We implemented our algorithm in C++. Intel SSE instructions are used in distance functions.

6. Experimental Results

Experimental platform

All test results reported in this paper were done on a desktop computer with following components:

CPU: Intel Core i5-2500K CPU (3.3GHz)

Memory: 16G

Operating System: Windows 7

Test Data Set

We use 3 different distributed data sets for testing:

- Uniform distribution in unit hypersphere (HS for short)

- Uniform distribution in unit hypercube (Cube for short)

- Regular Simplex(RS for short)
  points are random combination of vertexes of a d dimensional regular simplex.

Comparison Method

For Basic Bouncing Bubble algorithm, since the computational complexity is the same as Ritter's algorithm, so we will not compare the execution time. Instead, we will compare the precision of the results provided by both algorithms.

For Pruning Bouncing Bubble algorithm, we will not provide direct comparison with Kumar's algorithm or Fischer's algorithm. Kumar provided a test result on Matlab, which is incomparable with our implementation. However, Fischer provided a test result showing its algorithm's superiority over Kumar's. Thus we only need to compare with Fischer's algorithm.

Fischer's algorithm is an exact solver. To compare with it, we set precision as 10^{-6}, which is close to float precision limit and almost indistinguishable with exact solution in most applications.

Fischer's test results were done on a 400Mhz Sun Ultra 4 workstation. However, platform difference could not explain the huge performance difference (over 10^3 times in some cases) in execution time.

Basic Bouncing Bubble

We proposed Basic Bouncing Bubble as a substitution of Ritter's algorithm, thus we compared the error of results from both algorithm. As shown as follows:

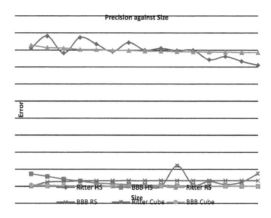

Fig 10 Precision comparison (against Size, dimension = 16)

In this test case, each test result is average from 10 independent tests (the same below). As we can see, our algorithm produce more precise results than Ritter's. The only exception is uniform distribution points in hypercube, to which Ritter's algorithm produce similar result with ours.

Test against dimension shows similar results, as shown as follows:

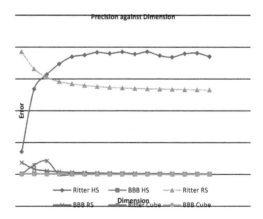

Fig 11 Precision comparison (against dimension, size = 30k)

Since it's relatively easy to handle uniform distribution point set in Hypercube, the following test were done only on uniform distribution point set in Hypersphere and Regular Simplex cases.

As an observation, Basic Bouncing Bubble algorithm produce coarser results for small data set in low dimensional space, which has important applications in computational graphic. Thus we conducted an extra comparison in such case.

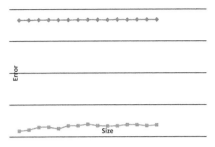

Fig 12 Precision Comparison (small data set, d=2)

In this case, our algorithm produce results with less than 2% error.

As we can see, Bouncing Bubble algorithm produce much precise results in nearly the same time Ritter's algorithm requires. Thus we can use Bouncing Bubble algorithm as a substitution of Ritter's algorithm.

Pruning Bouncing Bubble algorithm

Fig 1 shows an example of 2 dimension MEB problem. The data set D15112 [8] is taken from STPLIB, it consists 15112 locations of German cites. It takes only 0.025 second to complete the computation of $\epsilon=10^{-4}$.

Other experimental results are listed below:

We executed performance experiment against the size of data set, the dimension of the space and required precision.

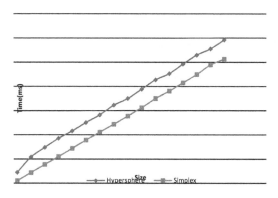

Fig 13 Performance against size (ε = 0.001, dimension = 16)

As shown in the figure, the execution time is linear against the size of the data set. However, as we can see in latter cases, execution time become insensitive to the size when ε is very small (e.g. $\epsilon = 10^{-6}$).

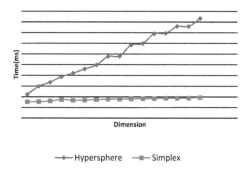

— Hypersphere — Simplex

Fig 14 Performance against dimension (ε = 0.001, size = 30000)

The execution time is also linear against the dimension. One noticeable point is the execution time for regular simplex case is almost const. This is because the points are concentrated in the centre area and thus been pruned in earlier stage.

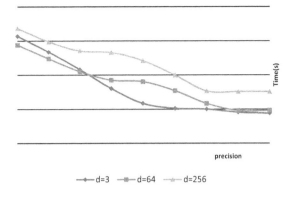

— d=3   — d=64   — d=256

Fig 15 Performance against required precision (size = 50k)

The above figure shows the execution time as a function against required precision (both axes in logarithmic scale). The test data set is uniform distributed points in unit hypersphere. Although worse case time complexity suggest execution time depends on $1/\epsilon^2$, the above plot of experimental results suggest the execution time has weak dependency on $(1/\epsilon)$.

Finally, we made some large case comparison, as shown as follows:

	Algorithm	Size	Dimension	Precision	Time(seconds)
1	Fischer	2000	2000	Exact	3500
2	Pruning Bouncing Bubble	2000	2000	10^{-6}	141
3	Pruning Bouncing Bubble	131072	2048	10^{-6}	226
4	Pruning Bouncing Bubble	262144	1024	10^{-6}	129
5	Pruning Bouncing Bubble	262144	1024	10^{-3}	5.6

The largest case is only limited by memory we can allocate one process in the platform, which is 1G bytes.

In the above table, we also provide an experimental result for precision 10^{-3} as a comparison. As high precision may not be critical in all application, ability to have tradeoff between precision and time saved is also essential.

Compare row 4 with row 3, we can see that the execution time is insensitive to the size of the data set but linear on the dimension, which is as suggested by the time complexity analysis.

7. Conclusion

In this paper, new approximation algorithms are proposed for minimal enclosing ball problem -- one simple algorithm as a substitution of Ritter's algorithm and one 1+ε approximation to provide arbitrary precision in less time.

Reference

1. K. Fischer, B. Gärtner and M. Kutz: Fast Smallest-Enclosing-Ball Computation in High Dimensions (2003)

2. P. Kumar, J.S.B. Mitchell and E.A Yıldırım: Computing Core-Sets and Approximate Smallest Enclosing HyperSpheres in High Dimensions (2003)

3. E. Welzl: Smallest Enclosing Disks (balls and ellipsoids) (1991)

4. B. Gärtner: Fast and Robust Smallest Enclosing Balls (1999)

5. M. Bădoiu, S. Har-Peled, and P. Indyk. Approximate clustering via core-sets. Proc. 34th Annu. ACM Sympos.on Theory of Computing, pages 250–257, 2002.

6. J. Ritter. An efficient bounding sphere. In Andrew S. Glassner, editor, Graphics Gems. Academic Press, Boston, MA, 1990.

7. Egecioglu and B. Kalantari. Approximating the diameter of a set of points in the Euclidean space. Information Processing Letters, 32:205-211, 1989.

8. http://neumann.hec.ca/chairelogistique/data/TSPPDL-VNS/d15112.tsp

www.ingramcontent.com/pod-product-compliance
Lightning Source LLC
Chambersburg PA
CBHW031234050326
40689CB00009B/1611